WORLD BOOK
Reading Development Program

LEVEL 6   Book 1

D1287703

World Book–Childcraft International, Inc.
A subsidiary of The Scott & Fetzer Company
Chicago London Sydney Tokyo Toronto

© 1981 by Reader's Digest Services, Inc.
Pleasantville, N.Y. 10570
All rights reserved, including the right
to reproduce this book or parts thereof in any form.
Printed in the United States of America

The credits and acknowledgments that appear
on the inside back cover are hereby made a
part of this copyright page.

ISBN 0-7166-3143-1

CONTENTS

NC 100

THE MYSTERY OF THE BERMUDA TRIANGLE

by James Stewart-Gordon

At 2:10 p.m. on December 5, 1945, five U.S. Navy training planes took off in clear weather from Fort Lauderdale, Florida. The planes flew east over the coast—and disappeared. The group was Flight 19, on a run between Florida and the Bahamas. Lieutenant C.C. Taylor was the group leader.

At about 3:40, Taylor reported that his compasses were not reading properly. The other pilots followed their leader aimlessly, first east, then west, then northeast over the ocean, as Taylor tried to get his bearing by radio. Then, suddenly, Taylor was heard to give orders to ditch.

Quickly, two giant Martin seaplanes were sent up to search for Flight 19. Several hours later, the wind became strong and visibility dropped. A return to base was ordered. Only one of the Martin seaplanes landed. For days after, the Navy and Coast Guard combed a 100,000 square-mile (258,998.8 square kilometers) area with more than 100 planes and ships. No trace was ever found of the missing planes.

Today, more than 30 years later, Flight 19 is at the center of a mystery that has given chills to people the world over. Magazines, books, newspapers, radio talk shows and TV specials have noted the disappearance of many ships and planes in the southwestern part of the North Atlantic. People have begun calling this area the Bermuda Triangle.

The points of the Triangle are Bermuda, Puerto Rico and a spot in the Gulf of Mexico west of Florida. It is a two-faced water world of tiny islands, bright beaches and beautiful waters. Yet thick hazes, powerful currents and sudden storms lurk behind this smiling surface. And one can never know, it seems, when the smile may turn into a snarl.

Of the 40 ships and 20 planes said to have been lost here during the last 100 years, 21 have met misfortune in December and January. That is when the Christmas Winds blow across the Triangle.

On December 5, 1946—exactly one year after Flight 19 disappeared—a pleasure ship, the *City Belle,* was found south of the Bahamas, deserted by its crew.

It was in January of 1958 that the Triangle is said to have swallowed up the yacht *Revonoc* with its owner and crew. They were going from Key West to Miami. The only traces of the *Revonoc* were pieces of a lifeboat and a toilet seat.

Another puzzling case happened on December 22, 1967. The owner of the 23-foot *Witchcraft* set out from Miami to view the city's Christmas lights. A few hours later, the owner radioed the Miami Coast Guard for assistance. His boat had a damaged propeller and was drifting near the harbor channel entrance. He reported that he could see Miami from the boat. Within ten minutes, the Coast Guard was on the spot. No sign of the boat was found then or since.

Planes have vanished in the air above the Triangle. In the summer of 1947, a U.S. Air Force Superfortress disappeared 100 miles (160.93 kilometers) from the Bermuda coast. On January 30, 1948, a British plane with 31 passengers aboard vanished after radioing Bermuda that all was well. In December 1948, the pilot of a DC-3 bound

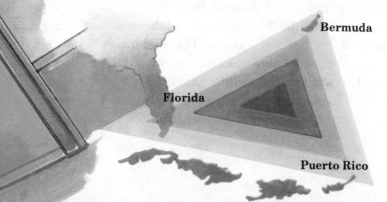

Bermuda

Florida

Puerto Rico

7

from San Juan to Miami reported the lights of Miami in sight. The passengers were singing Christmas carols. All was calm, all was bright—but the plane was never heard from again.

What happened to these ships and planes? Some people say that spaceships swooped down and gobbled up the ships and planes. Some believe the Triangle surrounds a giant tunnel leading to the center of the earth.

Others believe the mysteries can be explained by natural causes. For example, there is a logical explanation for the vanishing crew of the *City Belle*. Battered by a sudden storm, the ship radioed for help. The message was picked up by an American base, and the ship's crew was rescued.

The Straits of Florida are among the busiest waterways in the world. In the haze often found here, large ships sometimes run down smaller ones with no more than a light, unnoticed bump. From the bits found from the *Revonoc,* the Coast Guard thinks that is what could have happened to the unlucky boat.

The loss of the *Witchcraft* is another case that can be explained by natural causes. The night was windy. A damaged propeller slowed down the boat. The strong currents, the wind in the saillike canvas top, and the slower speed probably carried the boat north toward Ft. Lauderdale. From the sea, Ft. Lauderdale looks like Miami.

When *Witchcraft* radioed that it was off Miami, it was in fact off Ft. Lauderdale. The Coast Guard was looking in the wrong place. Eventually *Witchcraft* must have been carried out to sea.

Even long-time pilots can run into trouble in such an unpredictable area. The Superfortress that vanished in 1947 must have run into a storm and been destroyed.

Explaining the lost DC-3 and its Christmas singers, a Coast Guard captain says: "Before takeoff the pilot reported that his radio batteries were weak. Then the wind shifted strongly. Instead of being over south Florida, he was probably over the Gulf of Mexico and mistaking the lights of Key West for Miami. Finally he ran out of gas and crashed."

Flight 19 was lost not because of supernatural forces but because Taylor lost his bearings. Had he switched to his clear emergency radio channel, shore stations could have helped him find his position. Finally, panic seems to have taken over the pilots.

As for the lost Martin seaplane, a freighter reported a great, fiery bang at 7:50 p.m. in the area where the plane was flying. These seaplanes were known to develop loose fuel lines in rough air and then blow up. This seems to be the answer to this plane's mystery.

Captain Lonsdale of the Coast Guard sums up: "An average of 352 major ships a year are lost throughout the world. Four or five of these are hit so suddenly that they have no time to send out an S.O.S. If a ship is lost in what is known as the Bermuda Triangle, the Coast Guard considers it a disaster. To someone who doesn't know the facts, it seems unbelievable. I guess anything you can't understand yourself is bound to be supernatural."

WHAT HAPPENED? *cause/effect*

Match each mysterious disappearance in the Bermuda Triangle with the explanation given in the selection. Put the letters in the blanks.

Disappearance	*Explanation*
____ The *City Belle* was found south of the Bahamas, deserted by its crew.	a. In the haze, large ships run down smaller ships.
____ The Triangle swallowed up the *Renovoc*.	b. The boat owner told the Coast Guard the wrong location.
____ When the Coast Guard reached the spot, there was no sign of the *Witchcraft*.	c. This kind of plane is known to develop loose fuel lines in rough seas and then to blow up.
____ Five training planes in Flight 19 disappeared.	d. The leader lost his bearings. Panic took over the pilots.
____ A Martin seaplane disappeared.	e. The crew had been rescued.

☞ 155 • *Each correct answer 10 points* • *My Score* ____

SAVE THE FACTS   *fact/opinion*

Put 1 before each sentence that expresses an opinion, 2 before each sentence that expresses a fact.

____ The Triangle surrounds a giant tunnel leading to the center of the earth.

____ The *City Belle* was found deserted in 1946.

____ The *Witchcraft* has never been found.

____ All the mysterious disappearances in the Bermuda Triangle can be explained by natural causes.

10

———— Each year an average of 352 major ships are lost throughout the world.

☞ 131 · Each correct answer 5 points · My Score ————

SIGNALS   *author's purpose*

Why did the author write this story? Circle the numerals of two messages that the author wanted to give.

1. The disasters in the Bermuda Triangle can't be explained.
2. Many planes and ships have disappeared in the same area of the Atlantic Ocean.
3. Many mysteries in the Bermuda Triangle can be explained by natural causes.
4. All reports about the missing ships and planes are lies.

☞ 12 · Each correct answer 5 points · My Score ————

RESCUE THE MEANING   *phrase meaning*

The author described the Triangle as "two-faced water world of tiny islands." Underline three sentences that say almost the same thing.

1. The islands are close together.
2. It can be beautiful and also dangerous.
3. It has bright beaches and beautiful waters.
4. The seas are filled with unexpected hazards.
5. Sudden storms lurk behind the smiling surface.

☞ 77 · Each correct answer 5 points · My Score ————
Perfect Total Score 100 · My Total Score ————

A MYSTERY?   *opinions*

The author gave many explanations for the strange events within the Bermuda Triangle. Do you believe all the explanations? Do you believe there is something supernatural about the Triangle? Give reasons for your answers.

11

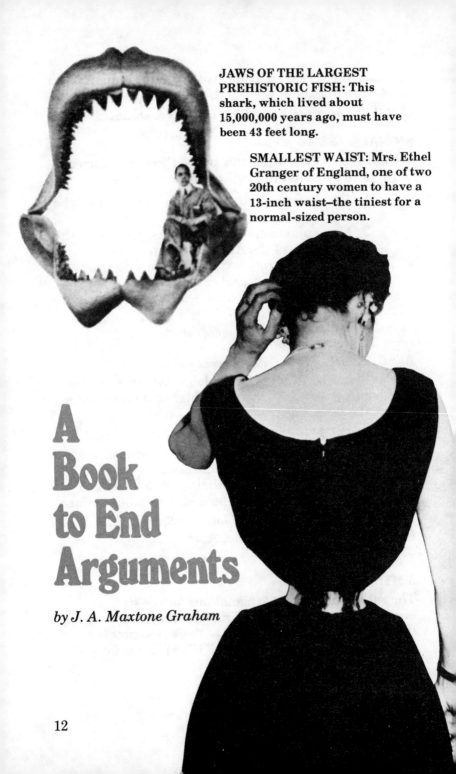

JAWS OF THE LARGEST PREHISTORIC FISH: This shark, which lived about 15,000,000 years ago, must have been 43 feet long.

SMALLEST WAIST: Mrs. Ethel Granger of England, one of two 20th century women to have a 13-inch waist—the tiniest for a normal-sized person.

A Book to End Arguments

by J. A. Maxtone Graham

It had been raw and windy on the Irish coast that winter day in 1954. A small flock of golden plover had come streaking past. They shot over the heads of a group of hunters. That evening the hunters sat by a crackling fire, reviewing the day's events.

"Those plover, they do move," said Sir Hugh Beaver, managing director of Arthur Guinness, Son & Co., Ltd., *brewers* (makers of beer). "Fast bird, I should say."

"But surely not as fast as a grouse with a tailwind," said someone else.

"Oh yes, far faster. The plover must be the fastest bird we've got. In fact—"

The argument continued with no winners, which is the case with most sporting discussions. But this one was going to have a remarkable result.

Sir Hugh returned to London. There he tried to find the speed of the fastest bird. He read encyclopedias and reference books, but no book had the answer.

"Why isn't there such a book," thought Sir Hugh. A book telling about the fastest, longest, tallest, oldest anything. A book of records. And why didn't Guinness, the largest brewer in Europe, publish it? Arguments break out all the time in Britain's *pubs* (taverns). The book would

LONGEST VENOMOUS SNAKE: The king cobra, 18 feet 9 inches long.

13

help some people win those arguments. Those people would be grateful to the Guinness company.

Sir Hugh asked one of his friends who might put such a book together. The friend replied immediately, "The McWhirter twins, of course."

Most people don't care if a race was won in 46.3 seconds or 46 seconds flat. But some people care a lot and will spend hours looking things up. Norris and Ross McWhirter were true "looker-uppers."

The McWhirter brothers had their own business. They supplied writers and editors with the answers to questions. They turned up facts such as the World's Heaviest Living Man (882 pounds/400.068 kilograms) and the Longest Chorus Line (Rockettes). Questions about the Tallest Television Mast (2063 feet/628.8024 meters, KTHI-TV, Fargo, N.D.) were no trouble for the twins.

The McWhirters agreed to do *The Guinness Book of World Records*. They wrote thousands of letters to museums and libraries.

The book was first published in 1955. Children from 8 to 80 were amazed by the facts they read. They were also spreading the news to their friends that the Land Speed Record was 632 miles per hour (1017.06 kilometers per hour) in a rocket sled.

The McWhirters have put out more than 12 editions of the book. They have sold millions of copies.

Sports records take up a large part of the book. One unusual sports record was set by Kenneth H. H. Baily. His hobby is running, often at night. Baily has run at least 157,295 miles (253,141.13 kilometers) in more than 45 years. He has never been run down by a car, but twice he has suffered attacks by owls.

The McWhirter brothers are helped by a small staff that turns up unusual facts. For instance, the Oldest Liv-

14

ing Thing is a bristlecone pine tree in California. It is 4617 years old.

There is a record for speed in smashing pianos and passing the broken bits through a nine-inch (22.86-centimeter) ring. That record was set by Johnny Leydon, an Englishman, and five helpers. Their time: 2 minutes, 26 seconds.

Then there is the record for the Fastest Climbing of the Stairs in the Empire State Building. It was done in 21 minutes in 1932 by the Polish Olympic Ski Team.

How about the Insect with the Best Sense of Smell? It's the male silkworm moth. It can smell another moth 6.8 miles (10.94 kilometers) away.

As you can tell, the record book is a most remarkable work. Sir Hugh Beaver now can find out the Fastest Bird. It is the spurwing goose (88 miles per hour/141.6 kilometers per hour). What about the plover? Sorry, Sir Hugh, no mention of it.

LIFTS MORE THAN THREE TONS: Paul Anderson, who weighs 364 lbs., raised the greatest weight ever lifted by a human being–6,270 lbs.–in a back lift.

OLDEST PERSON: Delina Filkins (U.S.) died in 1928, aged 113 years 214 days.

LOOK IT UP *skimming*

From the list below, circle the letter of the answer that best completes each sentence. You may need to look up the answer in the story.

1. The fastest bird flies (a. 88, b. 89, c. 106) miles per hour.
2. *The Guinness Book of World Records* was put together by (a. Arthur Guinness, b. Norris and Ross McWhirter, c. Sir Hugh Beaver).
3. The World's Heaviest Man weighs (a. 605, b. 848, c. 882) pounds.
4. The Polish Olympic Ski Team climbed the stairs of the Empire State Building in (a. 11, b. 14, c. 21) minutes.
5. The Land Speed Record is (a. 632, b. 1097, c. 1632) miles per hour.

☞ *133 • Each correct answer 5 points • My Score* _____

FIND THE FACTS *fact/opinion*

Some sentences below express facts. Other sentences express what the author believes, but may or may not be true. Put A before each statement that is a fact and B before each opinion.

_____ Johnny Leydon plays the piano well.
_____ The Oldest Living Thing is a tree in California.
_____ *The Guinness Book of World Records* is a most remarkable book.
_____ Kenneth H. H. Baily has run at least 157,295 miles in more than 45 years.
_____ The fastest bird is the spurwing goose.

☞ *130 • Each correct answer 5 points • My Score* _____

FOR THE RECORD *phrase meaning*

Read each italicized phrase. Then circle the letter of the answer that means nearly the same thing.

16

1. The birds *shot over the heads* of a group of hunters.
   a. flew quickly over
   b. fired their squawks over the hunters
   c. were fired at while flying over

2. "Those plover, they *do move.*"
   a. fly south during the winter
   b. can fly very quickly
   c. are nervous and always in motion

3. Norris and Ross McWhirter *were true "looker uppers."*
   a. watched things in the sky
   b. admired many other people
   c. searched out the answers to questions in books

☞ 49 · *Each correct answer 10 points* · *My Score* _____

SETTLE THE ARGUMENT   *supporting details*
One sentence below expresses the main idea of the story.
The other sentences support this main idea. Put 1 before
the main idea, 2 before the supporting details.

_____ *The Guinness Book of World Records* contains
many unusual facts.
_____ Children were amazed by the facts they read.
_____ Sports records take up a large part of the book.
_____ A team smashed a piano and passed the bits
through a ring in 2 minutes, 26 seconds.

☞ 87 · *Each correct answer 5 points* · *My Score* _____
Perfect Total Score 100 · *My Total Score* _____

WHERE DO I LOOK?   *classification/outline*
Imagine that you are one of the McWhirters. You are
about to begin work on *The Guinness Book of World
Records.* What books might you use to look up facts and
other information?

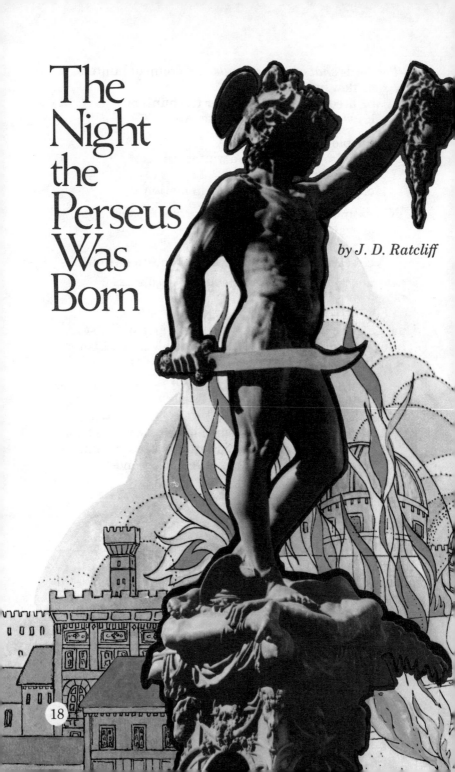

The Night the Perseus Was Born

by J. D. Ratcliff

A great *caldron* (pot) of melting copper glows in the darkness, lighting the faces of the ten men who watch. The wind howls, driving rain into the open-sided shed. Sparks fly from the roof, now on fire. On his bed in the adjoining house, a bearded, 49-year-old man with piercing eyes and a fierce look lies burning with fever, groaning, "I am dying."

This scene in 1549 marked the birth of one of the world's most admired masterpieces—Benvenuto Cellini's (ben-ve-NEW-toe chel-LEE-nee) bronze Perseus (PER-see-us). By a strange chain of circumstances, the full story of what happened that wild night has just come to light.

Cellini was a hot-tempered street fighter, ready to settle any argument by the sword.

Yet this strange man of Florence, Italy, had another side. The greatest goldsmith of his time, he made things out of gold which excited even the greatest artists of the day. He was a high-spirited companion, and generous to his friends. When his sister's husband died, he supported his sister and her six daughters. He saw to it that his aging father lived in comfort. He often helped others in need.

Beginning his life story, Cellini wrote: "I feel that all great people should tell the story of their lives, and so I am telling mine." He wanted to be sure that history would remember him. How could he do this? Sculpture seemed to be the answer. Sculptures 2000 years old are still cherished.

Cellini's big chance came in August of 1545. He rode to the summer castle of Grand Duke de'Medici (MED-ee-chee), a true lover of art. The Medici family had great wealth and power. They saw themselves as standing alone in saving the people of Florence from bad government. The Medici had cleverly used the arts to express this idea.

Now the Grand Duke's thoughts were on Perseus, a gallant character in Greek mythology. Perseus had done the impossible by beheading the Medusa (meh-DOO-sah), who had writhing snakes for hair and who was so terrible to see that anyone looking upon her was turned to stone. Like a clever Medici, the brave Perseus tricked Medusa.

Step 1 · Clay model made　　　*Step 2 · Model coated with wax*

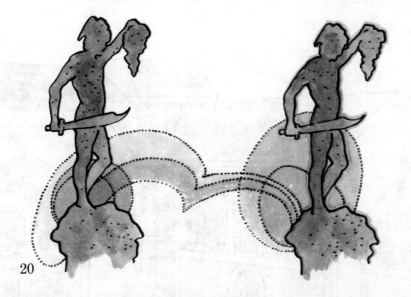

While they battled, Perseus simply looked at Medusa's reflection in a polished shield that he used as a mirror. The Grand Duke wanted a statue of Perseus to stand in the center of Florence, a symbol of Medici cleverness.

The idea of making a statue of Perseus suited Cellini perfectly. What could be better for keeping Cellini's name alive through history? Within a few weeks, Cellini returned to the Grand Duke with a small wax model showing Perseus in victory, holding Medusa's head high, his foot planted on Medusa's headless body. The Grand Duke was delighted and told Cellini to make the full-size statue.

Cellini kept putting off the work. In four years he found time only to sculpt and cast the headless Medusa. By the autumn of 1548, he had not yet begun to sculpt the hero, Perseus. The Grand Duke would wait no longer. He demanded that Cellini get to work.

With clay, sand, animal hair and iron, Cellini modeled a nine-foot (2.7-meter) Perseus. Next he coated this model

Step 3 • Clay-sand mold baked for two days

Step 4 • Bronze poured

21

with wax, making the wax exactly as thick as he wanted the bronze casting to be. The final step was to put more clay-sand over the wax, then bake the whole thing for two days. As the clay baked hard, the wax melted away, leaving a hollow mold into which Cellini could pour the bronze.

The Grand Duke visited the shop often. "Wouldn't it be better," he asked, "if a professional did the final casting?" Cellini had never done a job of such size. Cellini was furious. He could do anything! Yet even Cellini was worried—but for reasons that wouldn't appear for four hundred years!

When the time for casting came, a two-part furnace was built in Cellini's workshop. Cartloads of pine logs were brought in. The Perseus mold was buried in a pit beside the furnace so that the melted bronze could be channeled into it. Finally everything was ready. Blocks of metal were piled in the furnace to be melted.

For two days and two nights, workers kept the fire blazing. The little shop became an inferno, but the metal would not melt. The roof caught fire. (A rainstorm put it out.) The inside of the furnace began to crumble. (Make-do patching saved the day.) Still the metal refused to melt.

To add to his troubles, Cellini was suddenly struck down with a fever and had to leave the overseeing of the work to his most trusted helper. The artist went to his bed next door, saying his death was near at hand.

Finally a worker came into Cellini's room and said all was lost, the metal had *curdled* (became too thick to pour). Like a madman, Cellini leaped from his bed and

roared into the shed. The artist raged at everything in sight—the weather, wet logs, the workers—and went back to work. He sent helpers to get a load of dry oak firewood. He ordered carpets hung over the open side of the shed to keep out the cooling wind.

Bronze is made of copper and tin. It is the tin that makes the mixture flow. There was half a block of tin left. It went into the mixture. The metal began to move and glow. "I had brought the dead back to life!" wrote Cellini.

It was now four o'clock in the morning. Suddenly, with a great roar and a glowing light, the furnace lid blew open. At once, the plugs were knocked off to let the bronze pour—but it did not pour quickly enough!

In one last move, Cellini sent workers running to his house for his pewter plates, which were mostly tin. He

threw them in, and finally a hissing golden stream started flowing into the Perseus. The melted metal exactly filled the mold—there was hardly a drop left. Cellini fell on his knees and gave thanks.

After two days, the outside mold had cooled and was removed. It was a good casting job, but much work remained: filing, smoothing, filling air holes. Cellini wanted to add gold to the wings that were on Perseus' feet and helmet. It would take him another five years to do these finishing touches.

By April 27, 1554, the job was finished and the Perseus was given its first public showing on the spot where it stands today. Citizens flocked to see the statue, writing poems of praise which they pasted around the square. Even the Grand Duke decided that Perseus had been worth the trouble—though now the greedy Cellini wanted more than the agreed-upon price for the sculpture.

But why did Cellini have so much trouble pouring the

Perseus—a simple job for skilled workers? The answer did not come until after World War II. In 1942, fearing air raids, people stored Perseus in a basement. The job of putting it back after the war, and making a few small repairs, fell to Bruno Bearzi, one of the world's expert metal workers.

As Bearzi made the repairs, he kept wondering why Cellini had met with so much trouble with the pouring. Statue bronze is made with 10% tin and 90% copper. A proper 10%–90% mixture melts at about 850°F (454.4°C), which a log fire reaches easily. But if less tin is used, a much higher temperature is needed.

Bearzi searched through old records and found that Cellini had received the right amount of copper and tin for the job. But Bearzi had an idea. To check the idea, he chipped a tiny piece of bronze from under Perseus' curly hair, where it would not be seen. He had the bronze tested. The report showed the Perseus contained not 10% tin, but 1.7%!

That explained the near-disaster. Cellini was trying to cast a statue with almost pure copper, something which is nearly impossible. Of the valuable tin Cellini had received, less than a third was in the Perseus. Knowing Cellini's ways, Bearzi guessed that whenever the artist needed money, he simply sold some of the Grand Duke's tin.

Bearzi wrote a book about his discovery. The book told the 400-year-old secret of Perseus and proved again that Benvenuto Cellini was one of the greatest artists— and scoundrels—in history.

MOLD THE STORY *supporting details*

Read each group of sentences below. In each group, put 1 before the main idea. Put 2 before the supporting details.

Group A

_____ The metal should have poured, but it curdled.

_____ A proper 10%–90% mixture of tin and copper melts at 850° F.

_____ Bearzi kept wondering why Cellini had so much trouble with the pouring.

Group B

_____ In four years Cellini found time only to sculpt and cast the headless Medusa.

_____ If the Grand Duke was expecting to see the work finished soon, he was disappointed.

_____ Cellini kept putting off the work.

☞ *177 · Each correct answer 5 points · My Score* _____

CELLINI *characterization*

Decide what each sentence tells you about the character of Benvenuto Cellini. Circle each correct answer.

1. He was ever ready to settle any dispute by sword.
   a. hot-tempered b. greedy c. strong d. shy

2. He made things which excited even the greatest artists of the day.
   a. lazy b. violent c. strong-willed d. artistic

3. Cellini leaped from his bed and roared into the shed.
   a. happy b. furious c. weak d. confused

4. He wanted to be sure that history remembered him.
   a. wise b. proud c. angry d. depressed

5. Of the valuable tin Cellini had received, less than a third was put into Perseus.
   a. generous b. scared c. stupid d. greedy

6. When his sister's husband died, Cellini took it upon
himself to support his sister and her six daughters.
     a. courageous b. foolish c. generous
     d. unbalanced

☞ *190 • Each correct answer 5 points • My Score* ____

FINDING FACTS   *fact/opinion*

Put A before each sentence that is a fact. Put B before
each sentence that is an opinion.

____ 1. For two days and two nights, workers kept the
fire blazing.

____ 2. Cellini was the greatest goldsmith of his time.

____ 3. Citizens flocked to see the statue.

____ 4. There has never been anyone quite like Cellini.

____ 5. The Perseus was made for the Medici family.

____ 6. The Medici saw themselves as standing alone in
saving the people from bad government.

____ 7. The model for the Perseus statue was nine feet
high.

____ 8. Cellini was one of the greatest artists—and
scoundrels—in history.

☞ *218 • Each correct answer 5 points • My Score* ____
Perfect Total Score 100 • My Total Score ____

CELLINI ON TRIAL   *predicting*

Imagine that Bearzi had discovered and revealed Cellini's
secret when Cellini and the Grand Duke were still alive.
The Grand Duke had brought Cellini to court. The artist
is charged with the theft of the tin the Grand Duke had
given him for Perseus. What might Cellini say to defend
himself?

Althea!

The year was 1957. In parts of the United States, blacks could ride only in the backs of buses and sit only in theater balconies. They were barred from many restaurants. Separating blacks from other people was called *segregation*.

There was segregation in some tennis tournaments as well. In this climate one woman—one black woman—dared to be somebody. If it meant she would have to break through the color barrier of tennis, she was prepared to do it. Althea Gibson, long-legged super athlete from New York City, would be a champion tennis player.

Althea had the will, strength and reflexes of a great athlete. She was born with a dream to be a great athlete. But to make her dream come true, she would have to fight failure, disappointment, poverty and segregation.

by Phyllis Raybin Emert

From the beginning, sports came easily to her—basketball, baseball, handball. But she excelled in paddle tennis. By 1941, at age 13, Althea was New York's best paddle tennis player. People began to take notice.

After graduation from junior high school, she began devoting all her free time to tennis. Her free time came after work. The Gibson family was poor, and Althea wanted to help them. She worked in a factory and in a department store. She ran an elevator in a hotel and even had a job cleaning chickens in a butcher shop.

But after work she was free to follow her dream. She began taking tennis lessons from Fred Johnson, the one-armed tennis professional. She worked hard, and her game improved steadily. Soon she began to succeed. At 16 she won the Negro Tennis Association's Championship for Girls. To show the victory was no accident, she won it again the next year.

Her skill began attracting the attention of people who could help her. Dr. Hubert Eaton took Althea to live with his family in North Carolina. She attended the local high school and practiced tennis regularly on the doctor's court.

The next summer, Althea traveled the black tennis tournament circuit. She played in nine tournaments and won all nine. She also won the National Women's Singles title, which she held for nine years. Althea Gibson was now, without a doubt, the best woman player in black tennis.

Althea became a successful student as well as a successful athlete. After graduation from high school, the young tennis star won an athletic scholarship to Florida A & M. She played on the school's tennis and basketball teams. To earn money, she worked in the women's physical education department.

Althea with Queen Elizabeth

Still, this success did not satisfy Althea's dream. She was already the best black woman player. She wanted to be the best woman player—of any race. But first, she had to beat another opponent—segregation.

Blacks and whites had played in separate tournaments. Now Althea faced opposition as she began to break this color barrier. She wrote, "I will be accepted on my own merits, and that is the way I want it." Althea's merits as a person and athlete could not be denied. At Forest Hills in September 1950, Althea Gibson became the first black woman to play in the U.S. Open Tennis Tournament. She didn't win. But she almost scored a tremendous upset over champion Louise Brough.

The next year, she became the first black person to play at Wimbledon, England, the most famous and exciting of tennis tournaments. It was like playing in the World Series or Super Bowl. Though Althea did not win the tournament, she did win a victory. Now every color barrier in tennis had been broken.

In the autumn of 1955, the U.S. State Department asked Althea to represent her country on a six-week goodwill tour to foreign countries. She was excited by the idea.

The tour became a tremendous success for Althea. It was more satisfying and rewarding than anything she had yet done. She swept through 15 tournaments. Her six-week tour became eight months of repeated victories.

A year later she competed again at Wimbledon. She faced Darlene Hard in the finals. In front of Queen Elizabeth, and in blistering heat, Althea defeated Darlene in only 50 minutes. She became the first black person to win a major title at Wimbledon.

"It was no contest," *Time* magazine reported. "Ranging the court like a restless panther, Althea had her big game zeroed in with power and precision . . . ." A huge party was given for Althea, and she enjoyed every minute of it. She said, "It seems a long way from 143rd Street . . . shaking hands with the Queen of England . . . dancing with the Duke of Devonshire."

On her return to New York City, a large crowd met Althea at the airport. She rode in triumph back to her old neighborhood. Althea was given a ticker-tape parade down Broadway. The mayor of New York gave her a medallion of the city and held a luncheon in her honor.

Althea's victories continued, and within a year there was no question that she was the best woman tennis player in the world. Her dream and her talent had brought her, at last, to the top.

SERVE THE SEQUENCE *sequence*

Number the sentences in the order they happened in the story.

Althea . . .

_____ wins at Wimbledon.

_____ goes on a State Department goodwill tour.

_____ first wins the National Women's Singles title.

_____ graduates from Florida A&M.

☞105 · *Each correct answer 5 points · My Score* _____

MATCH THE MEANING *vocabulary*

Before each word in Column A, put the numeral of the word or phrase from Column B that means nearly the same thing.

Column A

_____ barrier

_____ medallion

_____ tournament

_____ merits

_____ reflex

_____ triumph

Column B

1. a large medal
2. something that separates
3. quickness of action
4. honor from a victory
5. good qualities
6. series of games

☞ 210 · *Each correct answer 5 points · My Score* _____

ACE THE FACTS *fact/opinion*

Some sentences below express facts. Other sentences express what the author believes, but may or may not be true. Put a check ✔ next to four statements of fact.

_____ 1. Separating blacks from other people was called segregation.

_____ 2. At 16, Althea won the Negro Tennis Association's Championship for Girls.

_____ 3. Althea's merits as a person and an athlete could not be denied.

_____ 4. Althea won an athletic scholarship to Florida A&M.

_____ 5. Wimbledon is the most famous and exciting of tennis tournaments.

_____ 6. At Forest Hills in September 1950, Althea Gibson became the first black person to play in the U.S. Open Tennis Tournament.

☞123 • *Each correct answer 5 points* • *My Score* _____

NET THE VIEWPOINT *points of view*

For each sentence below, decide whether the author approves or disapproves of the fact or idea expressed. Before each sentence, put 1 for approval and 2 for disapproval.

_____ There was segregation in some tennis tournaments.

_____ Althea became a successful student as well as a successful athlete.

_____ Althea wrote, "I will be accepted on my own merits, and that is the way I want it."

_____ Blacks and whites had played in separate tournaments.

_____ Althea faced opposition.

_____ Her dream and her talent had brought her, at last, to the top.

☞178 • *Each correct answer 5 points* • *My Score* _____
Perfect Total Score 100 • *My Total Score* _____

BREAK THE BARRIER *comparison/contrast*

How did Althea Gibson break the color barrier in tennis? How are some athletes today trying to break other barriers in sports? Give examples.

"TEACHER"

by Helen Keller

Before Anne Sullivan came to our house, one or two
people had told my mother that I was an idiot. I can
understand why. Here was a seven-year-old girl who at
the age of nineteen months had become deaf and blind.
And because I was deaf, I could not learn to speak. The few
baby words I had known were locked in my mind.
Struggling in a world of silence and darkness, I acted
almost like an animal.

But this was before Annie Sullivan came to stay. She was a lively young woman with patience and imagination. A born teacher, she dreamed of turning a deaf-blind creature into a useful human being.

What a challenge I presented to this young teacher! I remember her many attempts to spell words into my small hand. Annie used the manual alphabet, in which finger positions stand for letters. But neither words nor letters meant anything to me. I thought her finger movements were some kind of game. But at last, on April 5, 1887, she reached my understanding. About a month after her arrival, she taught me the word "water."

It happened at the well where I was holding a jug under the spout. Annie pumped the water, and as it gushed onto my hand, she kept spelling w-a-t-e-r into my other hand with her fingers. Suddenly I understood!

Caught up in the first joy I had known for years, I reached out to Annie's hand. She knew I was begging for new words to identify objects I touched. Spark after spark of meaning flew from her hand to mine.

From the well that April day walked two joyous people calling each other "Helen" and "Teacher." Those first words that I understood changed my world. Suddenly life crowded upon me, full of meaning.

One of Annie's first steps was to teach me how to play. I had not laughed since I became deaf. One day she came into my room laughing merrily. Putting my hand on her face, she spelled *l-a-u-g-h*. Then she tickled me into a burst of giggles. Next Annie led me through the motions of swinging, tumbling, hopping and skipping. She took care to spell the word for each act. In a few days I was learning—and laughing—like any child.

Annie kept some pigeons in a cage so that when they were let out I might feel the air from their wings. In this way I found out about the flight of birds. The pigeons would land on my head and shoulders. I learned to feed them and understand their pecking and fluttering. That is why birds, though unseen, have always been as much a part of my world as flowers and stones.

Teacher would not let the world about me be silent. I "heard" in my fingers the neigh of Prince, the saddle horse. I also "heard" the mooing of cows, the squeal of baby pigs. She brought me into touch with everything that could be reached or felt—sunlight, the quivering of soap bubbles, the rustling of silk, the noises of insects, the creaking of a door, the voice of a loved one.

Teacher showed me also how to handle everything gently—a canary, a rose with dew drops, my baby sister. I was awkward and clumsy, but she tamed my rough ways.

Annie disciplined me exactly as if I were a seeing and hearing child. As soon as I had enough words to know the difference between right and wrong, I was put to bed whenever I misbehaved. How wonderful to be treated like a normal child—even when I was bad!

As I look back upon those years, I am struck by Annie's wisdom. Perhaps she understood me because she herself had always had very weak eyes.

Annie was born in ugly poverty, on April 4, 1866. Her mother died when she was eight years old. Two years later, her father disappeared, never to be heard from again. Annie and her brother were sent to an orphanage. There the boy died.

No one outside the orphanage was interested in Annie. But finally, after four years, she managed to escape by crying out to a group of visitors, "I want to go to school!"

At the Perkins Institution for the Blind, Annie learned Braille. This is a kind of printing with raised dots

that blind people can read by touch. She also learned the manual alphabet.

Later, an operation partly restored her sight, but she remained at Perkins for six years more. There she studied about teaching deaf-blind children.

One day a letter from my father arrived at the school. It asked for a teacher for me. Annie considered the challenge just the one she wanted.

Teacher was among the first to realize that a sightless person never knows his hidden strength until he is treated like a normal human being. She never pitied me. She never praised me unless my effort equaled the best of a normal person. And she encouraged me when I made up my mind to go to college.

During my years in school, Annie sat beside me in every class. She spelled out the teachers' lectures. And,

Helen Keller at about age 13, with Anne Sullivan

because many books were not printed in Braille, she read them to me by spelling the information into my hand.

Teacher's eyes were always a problem. "I can't see an inch ahead," she once admitted. A doctor was shocked when he heard that she read to me five or more hours daily. "It is sheer madness, Miss Sullivan!" he exclaimed. Quite often I pretended to remember parts of books that had slipped my mind, so that she wouldn't have to reread them.

It took superhuman patience for Annie to teach me to speak. Putting both hands on her face when she spoke, she let me feel all the vibrations from her lips and throat. Together we repeated and repeated words and sentences. My speech was clumsy and not pleasant to hear. But I was delighted to be able to say words that my family and a few friends could understand. To Annie I owe thanks for this priceless gift of speech. It has helped me to serve others.

Teacher's inspiration lived on after her death. She had believed in me. I must always keep on trying to do my best.

"No matter what happens," she often said, "keep on beginning. Each time you fail, start all over again. You will grow stronger until you find that you have accomplished a purpose." And who could count the times Annie tried, failed, and then conquered?

ANNE AND HELEN   *classification/outline*

In the first column put a check ✔ next to words that describe Anne Sullivan. In the second column put a check ✔ next to words that describe Helen Keller.

Anne Sullivan   *Helen Keller*

_____ 1. patient   _____ 5. eager

_____ 2. determined   _____ 6. intelligent

_____ 3. pitying   _____ 7. shy

_____ 4. wise   _____ 8. grateful

☞ *215 · Each correct answer 5 points · My Score* _____

HELEN KELLER   *author's purpose*

Read each sentence below. Underline the word that best describes the author's feelings at the time.

1. Struggling in a world of silence and darkness, I acted almost like an animal.
     a. happy   b. helpless   c. proud
2. But neither words nor letters meant anything to me.
     a. proud   b. embarrassed   c. confused
3. She kept spelling w-a-t-e-r into my other hand with her fingers. Suddenly I understood!
     a. excited   b. puzzled   c. patient
4. During my school years, Annie sat beside me in every class.
     a. hopeless   b. grateful   c. annoyed

☞ *90 · Each correct answer 5 points · My Score* _____

ANNE SULLIVAN   *supporting details*

Put a check ✔ next to five sentences that support the idea that Anne was a good teacher for Helen.

_____ 1. One of Annie's first steps was to teach me how to play.

_____ 2. Annie was born in ugly poverty, on April 4, 1866.

_____ 3. Teacher would not let the world about me be silent.

_____ 4. Annie disciplined me exactly as if I were a seeing and hearing child.

_____ 5. It took superhuman patience for Annie to teach me to speak.

_____ 6. She encouraged me when I made up my mind to go to college.

☞ *168 · Each correct answer 5 points · My Score* _____

JUST THE FACTS   *fact/opinion*

Write A before each sentence that states a fact.
Write B before each sentence that tells what the author believes.

_____ 1. Helen Keller became deaf and blind at the age of nineteen months.

_____ 2. What a challenge I presented to this young teacher.

_____ 3. It was wonderful to be treated like a normal child.

_____ 4. At the Perkins Institution for the Blind, Annie learned Braille.

_____ 5. Perhaps she understood me because Annie herself had always had very weak eyes.

☞ *128 · Each correct answer 5 points · My Score* _____
Perfect Total Score 100 · My Total Score _____

THE TEACHER   *characterization*

What personal qualities did Annie develop as a result of her childhood? How did these qualities help her as Helen's teacher?

Tornado

by Angus Dale Wright

It is a hot, sticky day in spring on the Great Plains States of North America. As late afternoon approaches, the air becomes still and quiet. Clouds begin to gather as two great air masses meet silently in the sky above. Nature is about to unleash its awesome power.

Distant thunder signals the beginning of the conflict. As the warm moist air mixes with the cool dry air, thick black clouds begin to churn overhead. The crack of thunder becomes more intense as the lightning casts a green outline around the clouds. Rain and hail pelt the ground below. There is a race to close windows and doors . . . a fatal mistake.

Suddenly the bottoms of the black clouds heave downward like giant grapes hanging from a vine. One bulge lengthens into a snake-like coil racing down to the earth below. The deafening roar of a thousand moving freight trains fills the air. The funnel, now 400 yards (365.8 meters) across, rips into the ground as it twists trees out by the roots. Passing over a house, the roof jerks upward and tumbles into the growing mass of debris. Walls are blown apart as if hit by a mortar shell. Broken glass spirals around the core of the funnel at speeds up to 500 miles (804.7 kilometers) per hour. A tornado is born!

The word tornado is derived from a word meaning "to turn" and the Spanish word *tronada* meaning "thunderstorm". Tornados have been identified all over the world, yet the conditions in the Central Plains States are the most ideal for tornado formation.

The tornado is nature's smallest, but most violent storm. It is born from a thunderstorm when a cold dry layer of air from the Pacific Northwest meets a warm moist layer of air from the Gulf of Mexico. All tornados have a funnel-shaped cloud of very low pressure. The edges of the swirling funnel may have wind speeds approaching 500 miles (804.65 kilometers) per hour. The tornado looks like a giant twisting rope hanging down from the clouds above. The span of the funnel may range from 100 yards (91.44 meters) to more than half a mile in diameter. Generally the twister moves from the southwest to the northeast at speeds of 20 to 50 miles per hour (32.19 to 80.47 kilometers).

Few people have passed through a tornado and lived to tell about it. Those that have, describe the core of the storm as a hollow tunnel. The walls are made of swirling debris, dust, and water particles. Lightning flashes around the edges of the core, perhaps causing the great roar and hissing sounds that are always associated with the storm.

The unleashed fury of the tornado seldom leaves its victims a chance to escape. Two forces within the tornado lash out with devastating force. The first is the wind in the outer edge of the funnel. Speeds exceeding 500 miles (804.65 kilometers) per hour have been known to drive a straw through a metal fence. But the most damaging force is the low pressure of the funnel. Within seconds after the funnel passes over a house, the outside pressure drops drastically. It is as if a huge vacuum cleaner had just been thrust over the house. The trapped air inside tries to escape. Within seconds the inside air pushes outward on the closed windows with 4 or 5 tons (3.628 to 4.539 metric tons) of pressure. The pressure on walls and ceiling reaches a staggering 2000 tons (1814.00 metric tons), literally blowing the house apart. Then the tremendous speed of the rotating winds picks up the broken glass, wood, and bricks.

Once in the actual whirling mass of debris that makes up a tornado, survival is not probable. However, these violent storms are very small in size and last for a relatively short period of time. It is sometimes possible to outrun

the funnel. If the funnel can't be outrun, drop to the ground in the lowest depression you can find. Cover your head with your hands or a jacket. Sometimes, the funnel will hop right over a depression, leaving the occupant unharmed. Most cars can outrun tornados although tornados moving along at 125 miles (201.16 kilometers) per hour have been experienced. If you can't outrun the funnel, leave the car and drop low to the ground.

In a building, the real danger is from the crumbling debris blown apart by the low pressure. If time allows, throw open the doors and windows to let the inside air escape. Then seek shelter in the southwest corner of the basement. If the walls do crumble, they will generally be thrown into the northeast corner of the building. Twisters cover a very narrow band of the ground and generally recede back into the sky after traveling a few miles along the surface. If the tornado can be seen in the distance, you have a good chance of avoiding its fury.

TWISTER FACTS *skimming*

Circle the letter of the answer that best completes each sentence.

1. The edges of a tornado's funnel can have wind speeds up to (a. 500, b. 875, c. 1000) miles per hour.

2. Generally a tornado moves from (a. northwest to southeast, b. southeast to northwest, c. southwest to northeast).

3. Most tornados travel at speeds of (a. 10–20, b. 15–30, c. 20–50) miles per hour.

4. The most damaging force of a tornado is the (a. lightning at the edge, b. low pressure at the center, c. tidal waves formed).

☞ 89 · *Each correct answer 5 points · My Score* ____

FUNNEL OF WORDS *figurative language*

A *simile* is a comparison between things, as in *He roared like a lion.* Put a check ✔ next to three sentences below that use similes.

____ 1. Suddenly the bottoms of the black clouds heave downward like giant grapes hanging from a vine.

____ 2. The crack of thunder becomes more intense as the lightning casts a green outline around the clouds.

____ 3. Tornados have been identified all over the world, yet the conditions in the Central Plains States are the most ideal for tornado formation.

____ 4. Walls are blown apart as if hit by a mortar shell.

____ 5. It is as if a huge vacuum cleaner had just been thrust over the house.

☞ 76 · *Each correct answer 10 points · My Score* ____

TWISTER FURY *author's purpose*

Put a check ✔ next to four sentences the author used to show the power of a tornado.

48

_____ 1. The funnel rips into the ground as it twists trees out by the roots.

_____ 2. Broken glass spirals around the core of the funnel at speeds up to 500 miles per hour.

_____ 3. The word tornado is derived from a word meaning "to turn."

_____ 4. Few people have passed through a tornado and lived to tell about it.

_____ 5. All tornados have a funnel-shaped cloud of very low pressure.

_____ 6. Speeds exceeding 500 miles per hour have been known to drive a straw through a metal fence.

_____ 7. Twisters cover a very narrow band of the ground and generally recede back into the sky after traveling a few miles along the surface.

☞ 123 · _Each correct answer 5 points_ · _My Score_ _____

STORM WORDS   _vocabulary_

Circle the letter of the answer that could best replace each italicized word.

1. Rain and hail _pelt_ the ground below.
    a. beat   b. soak   c. color

2. The roof tumbles into the growing mass of _debris_.
    a. lights   b. walls   c. ruins

3. Then the tremendous speed of the _rotating_ winds picks up the broken glass, wood and bricks.
    a. howling   b. powerful   c. spinning

☞ 51 · _Each correct answer 10 points_ · _My Score_ _____
Perfect Total Score 100 · _My Total Score_ _____

ACTION   _generalizations_

Do any natural disasters such as tornados, hurricanes and earthquakes strike your area? If so, what has your community done to deal with the problem?

Green Against Gray

by Anne Ophelia Dowden

In the country the color of life is green, but a city is brown, black and gray. A big city spreads over the earth a crust of brick and concrete, metal and glass. Millions of people live and work and play in cities. Tall apartment houses and office buildings rise above paved streets and sidewalks. There is little breathing space in the city.

But look closely as you walk. Look at the cracks in the sidewalk, along the gutter's edge, around the edges of parking lots, in old railroad yards, along docksides, in vacant lots. You will find fresh green plants with flowers of pink, yellow, white, blue—a rainbow of colors.

These are the wild plants of a great city. They are often overlooked and trampled upon. But it is cheering to see a small dandelion fighting its way to sunlight in some empty lot. Or a milkweed breaking through asphalt with an urge to be alive. More than 90 kinds of "weeds" have been found in New York City, 60 in Denver, 130 in Los Angeles.

The plant life of any place depends on many factors working together—soil, air, light, rain, temperature, animal life. The soil must have water and minerals, which plants use in making food. The soil must be loose enough so water, air and roots can work down into it.

Yet city earth is packed hard. There are few spaces for water to collect around tiny pieces of soil. The city earth has few worms to tunnel through it, loosening the soil. Rainwater falling on this hard-packed city earth is likely to run off

51

before it can soak down to root level. Or it stands in puddles and threatens to drown roots and kill the plants.

What's more, city plants live in a constant fall of soot. Soot and the oily, black film that coats leaves can damage plants. The soot and dirt clog the breathing pores and screen out sunlight. The heavy blanket of smog that covers many cities has already shut out a good part of the natural sunlight. The air is full of chemicals that can burn plants.

How did plants get to the city in the first place? Growing plants spend their lives where they are rooted. But their seeds can travel long distances. The flying seeds of plants like milkweed, dandelion and goldenrod are carried on the wind. Millions of these seeds stick and grow in all kinds of places—even in the cracks of brick walls.

These flying seeds often have wings. Other seeds, such as beggar-ticks, catch in hair or clothing of people and hitch a ride to a new home.

Many of our wild city flowers can produce hundreds of new plants without seeds. Some plants send out runners from their roots from which new plants begin. Other plants, especially grasses, have stems which lie on the ground or travel underground. Wherever a leaf branches from these stems, roots may form and start a new plant.

City plants are strong. Against all odds, they can make new plants and spread to new places. Many of our weeds came to America from other lands. Settlers brought seeds or plants they had grown for food, medicine or pleasure. Clovers and grasses were brought to

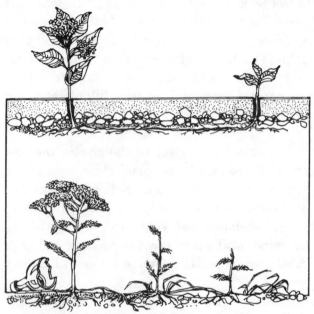

New plants being produced without seeds

America to feed cows and horses. And dozens of plants crossed to America in bales of hay, in packing and in earth that was used as ballast for ships.

Other weeds, of course, are native Americans. They, too, were given new chances as the countryside changed. These include some of the most beautiful plants found in city lots—sunflower, goldenrod, aster, milkweed. These plants have the strength that allows them to live even in the city. To add a touch of green against gray.

NEW PLANTS *skimming*

Put a check ✔ next to four methods by which a plant can "travel."

_____ 1. Flying seeds are carried on the wind.
_____ 2. The seeds catch on the hair or clothing of people.
_____ 3. Millions of new seeds are planted each year by city park workers.
_____ 4. Some plants send out runners from their roots.
_____ 5. Other weeds are native Americans.
_____ 6. The stems travel underground and new roots are formed.

☞ 123 · *Each correct answer 5 points · My Score* _____

AGAINST ALL ODDS *cause/effect*

Put a check ✔ next to six sentences that tell why it is hard for plants to grow in cities.

_____ 1. A big city spreads over the earth a crust of brick and concrete, metal and glass.
_____ 2. City earth is packed hard.
_____ 3. Growing plants spend their lives where they are rooted.
_____ 4. The city earth has few worms to tunnel through it.
_____ 5. The soot and dirt clog the breathing pores.
_____ 6. The heavy blanket of smog shuts out a good part of natural sunlight.
_____ 7. Many of our wild city flowers can produce hundreds of new plants without seeds.
_____ 8. The air is full of chemicals that can burn plants.

☞ 215 · *Each correct answer 5 points · My Score* _____

FLOWER POWER *author's purpose*

Check ✔ four sentences that tell you why the author wrote this article.

The author wanted to . . .

_____ 1. get more people to move to the country.
_____ 2. make city people aware of the plants around them.
_____ 3. show that even weeds can be beautiful.
_____ 4. have people plant more flowers in cities.
_____ 5. show that plants can grow even in hard environments.
_____ 6. give certain facts about city plants.

☞ 122 · *Each correct answer 5 points* · *My Score* _____

MORE GREEN *main idea*

In each set of sentences below, one sentence expresses the main idea. The other two sentences support the main idea. Put 1 before each main idea, 2 before each detail.

_____ The plant life of any place depends on many factors working together.
_____ The soil must have water and minerals.
_____ The soil must be loose enough so that water, air and roots can work down into it.

_____ Some plants send out runners from their roots from which new plants begin.
_____ Many of our wild city flowers can produce hundreds of new plants without seeds.
_____ Other plants have stems which lie on the ground or travel underground.

☞ 177 · *Each correct answer 5 points* · *My Score* _____
Perfect Total Score 100 · *My Total Score* _____

A TOUCH OF COLOR *points of view*

How do the wild flowers add a touch of color to a city? What other touches of nature are often overlooked in a city?

Roald Amundsen

by Emily and Ola d'Aulaire

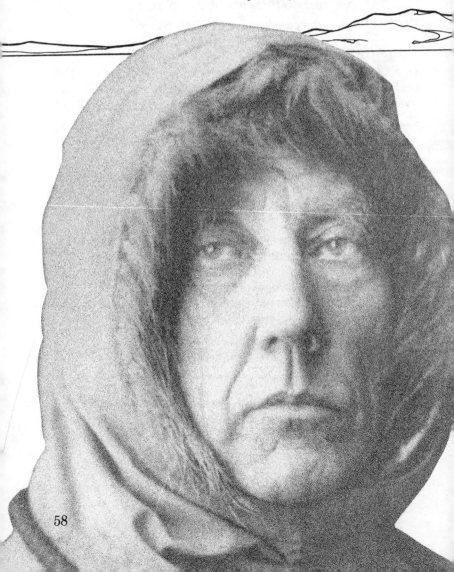

Polar Pioneer

The midnight sun glowed like a giant ember that January night in 1912. Five men crept into the small wood hut. Inside, the only sound was the even breathing that came from the bunks lining the walls. But as the newcomers began to peel off their layers of clothing, one by one the sleeping men awakened and gaped as if they were seeing ghosts. Finally one of the men whispered: "Have you been there?" The tallest of the newcomers slowly looked from man to man. He said, "Yes, we have been there."

In an instant, the hut was a turmoil of men shouting, laughing, leaping, hugging. The tall man who had spoken was Roald Amundsen, called by many the greatest polar explorer of all time. And the "there" was the very bottom of the world. It was an inhospitable circle of eternal ice and snow, never before visited by humans—the South Pole.

Roald was born at Borge, Norway, in July 1872. His father and uncles were shipowners, and young Roald had heard stories of distant lands and the sea. At 15, he read about Sir John Franklin's attempt to sail the Northwest Passage. The passage is an ice-choked waterway through the jumble of Canada's Arctic islands. Franklin and 129 men with him had died from hunger and the cold. Amundsen wrote, "The thing that appealed to me most was the suffering Sir John and his men had endured. I secretly vowed to become an explorer."

Six years later, Roald signed on as an ordinary sailor aboard a seal-hunting ship heading for the Arctic (North Pole). He learned the ways of seafaring quickly. At 25, he became the first mate of the ship of the Belgian Antarctic (South Pole) Expedition. The ship remained ice-bound in the Antarctic Ocean for 13 months. Its crew was the first ever to weather the Antarctic winter.

Once home, Amundsen began plans to sail the Northwest Passage. He studied everything written on earlier journeys. He studied Scandinavia's Laplanders to discover how they survived the cold. He learned how to handle dog teams and became an expert on cross-country skis. Finally, he bought an old ship, which he carefully stocked for the trip. Dried meat for five years and scientific gear went into special packing cases. The cases could double as building blocks for the land base they would need in winter. He chose only six men to go along, as it would be easier to feed them if stranded.

These long months of careful preparation almost wrecked the expedition. Amundsen had very little cash of his own. He owed money for almost all of his equipment. On June 16, 1903, his bankers demanded money within 24 hours, or they would take his ship. Amundsen knew he couldn't raise the needed money in time. So that night he and his crew silently sailed down the Oslo Fjord and on to high adventure.

Amundsen knew that most explorers before him had followed a northerly course. So in Lancaster Sound, in the Canadian Arctic, he headed due south. By the time the Arctic winter's ice closed in, Amundsen's ship had gone

The old herring sloop "Gjoa" with which Amundsen discovered the Northwest Passage in 1903-1905.

farther than any ship had before. On desolate King William Island, Amundsen's group built their packing-case houses and prepared for the long, icy season.

Their vessel remained in ice for two winters. Finally, in August 1905, the ice opened, and Amundsen steered the little vessel through the shallow waters off the shores of northern mainland Canada. Two weeks later, they sighted a ship in the west, a whaling ship from San Francisco. Wrote Amundsen, "What a glorious sight. It meant the Northwest Passage lay behind us."

When he got back home, Amundsen raised money giving speeches, paid his debts and prepared for his next venture. He would enter the Arctic north of Russia and drift west with the pack ice over the North Pole itself.

In September 1909, nearly prepared, he received a hard blow. U.S. Admiral Robert E. Peary had reached the North Pole ahead of him. Amundsen went about his business. If the North Pole was gone, why not make a dash for the South Pole?

From the very beginning, Amundsen's plan was brilliant. On reaching Antarctica, he built a wood hut onshore for men and supplies. Food, clothing and tools were stored in three places on the Ross Ice Shelf. The supplies would be used on the return trip from the South Pole.

When spring arrived, Amundsen and four men, with 52 Eskimo dogs and four sleds, began the 900-mile (1448.4-kilometer) trek to the Pole. In a month they reached the continental mountain range. From there it took four exhausting days to climb the 10,000 feet (3048 meters) to the Polar Plateau. There they were met by a screaming blizzard. Half blinded by the driving snow, the men fought their way on.

Finally, on December 14, 1911, at 3 p.m., they reached the very bottom of the world. They planted Norway's flag at the South Pole. It was a proud moment.

Amundsen's career was far from ended. He acquired a new ship and for four years tried in vain to enter the drifting North Pole. Finally he decided he would have to reach the North Pole by air. In 1925, his effort ended because of engine trouble. Amundsen had flown closer to the North Pole than had anyone before him, but he still had not reached it. Nor had anyone crossed the Arctic Ocean, going from Europe to America. In May of 1926, Amundsen took off in an airship built and flown by Umberto Nobile of Italy. Amundsen's lifelong dream came true as the huge silver-colored airship floated over the North Pole. He had done it—the first to cross the top of the world!

"I consider my career as an explorer closed," Amundsen said. But history was not through with him. Two years later, and on a different mission, Umberto Nobile's airship crashed on the polar ice. A rescue party had to be quickly organized to search for survivors. Amundsen, then 56 and aged beyond his years, said, "I know the area. I will go." On June 18, 1928, he took off on his mission of mercy—his last. For three months, the world clung to the faint hope that somehow he would return again—until the damaged float from his seaplane was found.

Careful planning, careful preparation, great physical endurance—these explain why Amundsen succeeded where others had failed. He said, "I did what I set out to do."

The Norwegian Flag on the South Pole, December 14, 1911.

dit: Norwegian Folks Museum

EXPLORE FOR FACTS   *story elements*

Underline the sentence ending that would help you recall important information.

1. Roald was born in (a. Norway, b. Denmark, c. England).

2. The Northwest Passage is a waterway that lies between (a. Russia and Alaska, b. England and France, c. Canada and the North Pole).

3. When Roald was 21, he (a. went on vacation to the South Pole, b. became captain, c. became a seaman aboard a seal-hunting ship).

4. Amundsen first crossed the North Pole (a. by dogsled, b. in an airship, c. on skis).

☞ 89 · *Each correct answer 5 points* · *My Score* _____

THE MAN BEHIND THE LEGEND   *characterization*

To help you picture the kind of person Roald Amundsen was, which of the following words did the authors use? Check ✔ four.

_____ 1. timid   _____ 5. careful
_____ 2. tall   _____ 6. proud
_____ 3. determined   _____ 7. inhospitable
_____ 4. weak   _____ 8. wealthy

☞ 122 · *Each correct answer 5 points* · *My Score* _____

DESTINATION: DANGER   *author's purpose*

The authors used four facts to show the dangers of Arctic exploration. Check ✔ each.

_____ 1. It was an inhospitable circle of eternal ice and snow never before visited.
_____ 2. "The thing that appealed to me most was the suffering Sir John and his men had endured."
_____ 3. Young Roald had heard stories of distant lands and the sea.

_____ 4. He studied Scandinavia's Laplanders to discover how they survived the cold.

_____ 5. He bought an old ship, which he stocked for the trip.

_____ 6. Dried meat for five years and scientific gear went into special packing cases.

☞ *123 • Each correct answer 5 points • My Score* _____

EXPLORER'S LIFE   *sequence*

Put the events of Amundsen's life in the correct order. Put 1 before the first event, 2 before the second and so on.

Roald Amundsen . . .

_____ learned the ways of seafaring.

_____ crossed the North Pole by airship.

_____ reached the South Pole.

_____ was first mate on the Belgian Antarctic Expedition.

_____ sailed through the Northwest Passage.

_____ read about Sir John Franklin.

☞ *213 • Each correct answer 5 points • My Score* _____

NOT LIKE EACH OTHER   *vocabulary*

In the story, three of the four words in each set have nearly the same meaning as the italicized word. Underline the word or phrase that does not belong.

Explore

     a. seek   b. lose   c. search   d. examine

Waterway

     a. canal   b. river   c. ocean   d. boat

☞ *21 • Each correct answer 5 points • My Score* _____
Perfect Total Score 100 • My Total Score _____

BE AN EXPLORER   *comparison/contrast*

How are the moon explorers like Roald Amundsen? How are they unlike him?

65

Cities in the Sky

by Richard Dempewolff

Picture a huge cylinder about 16 miles (25.7 kilometers) long and four miles (6.4 kilometers) across *orbiting* (flying in a circular path) in space. Inside, you step from your cozy little cottage, stroll down a flower-lined garden path, wander through bird-filled wildlands. You picnic in a forest park, swim in a lake, fish in a river. Later you ride your bicycle or a tiny electric car to the shopping center for groceries.

The cylinder will be spinning to make artificial *gravity* (the feeling of having weight). But you won't notice the turning. Everything will be just as it is on Earth. But there will be no crowds, no traffic jams, no honking car horns, no noise from heavy industry, no eye-smarting smoke. The air will be clean and fresh, with a shirt-sleeve climate.

At 8000 feet (2438.4 meters) high, you'll be able to pedal your own flying machine. This is because the "gravity" decreases as you near the center of the cylinder.

Living in this cylinder will have other strange effects. When you look across the four miles (6.4 kilometers) of

67

the cylinder's interior, you'll see your neighbors' homes upside down on the "roof." Water will run uphill.

You'll be able to swim and bask on beaches. You'll get a real suntan from real sunlight streaming in through long slots in the sides.

This bold plan to put whole colonies in space sounds like science fiction. But it isn't. Doctor Gerard K. O'Neill, the scientist who created the plan, says, "We can colonize space now. We know what to do and how to do it." If it were started now, O'Neill thinks the first colony would be ready by the late 1980s. In any case, space communities could be ready around the year 2000.

Each colony cylinder would be made of a weblike framework of cables and ribs. The cables would run from end to end, holding the end caps in place. Ribs would wrap around the cylinder like barrel hoops holding in

place six panels. Each of these six strips would be sixteen miles (25.7 kilometers) long and about two miles (3.2 kilometers) wide. Three of them—every other one—would be "land" areas, built up with real rock and soil. Any kind of land form can be made, from rolling hills to sweeping plains, from rain forests to deserts.

O'Neill explains that these cities would "fly" in pairs about 50 miles (80.4 kilometers) apart, joined by cables. He points out that it will be possible to give one cylinder a summer climate, while another could be like winter.

Crops will be raised outside the base cylinder in a ring of smaller cylinders. This will leave more living space in the large cylinder. Each small cylinder can be tailored to suit the specific thing growing there. Doctor Eric Hannah, O'Neill's right-hand man, says, "Each one can have its own climate and seasons, geared for fruit, chickens, winter wheat, cattle, whatever you want."

Other small cylinders would be used to house factories, workshops and laboratories. Such work would be safely away from where people are living. An animal or plant disease would be kept in check by sealing off the small cylinder. Many of the things made in the small cylinder would be sold on Earth. Power from satellite stations could also be sold to Earth.

The space colonies will circle the Earth along the same path as the moon. Each pair of space cities would be spread out from the other pair along these paths about 120 miles (193.1 kilometers) apart. This would be far enough apart for safety, yet close enough for easy access to each other. Public space "buses" would make regular trips between cities. To get to your twin city, you would get into a small craft locked to the outside of your city. Then it would be flipped into space by your city's spin at about 400 miles (643.7 kilometers) an hour. In nine minutes, you would lock onto a docking tower at the nose of your twin city, where flights from Earth also "land."

The space cylinders will be filled with air and heated. They will allow work to be done inside in light clothes rather than in heavy space suits. These giant space cities will not only be built in space, but will largely use material and energy sources found in space. Power will come from the sun. Ore will come from the moon. Moving ore from the moon to a space city will take only 5% the energy needed to move it there from Earth.

Such space colonies could be of great help for the Earth itself. They could ease the pressure of too many people. Once factories can run in space, the Earth's air and water would start cleaning up. Space stations making electricity from the sun could beam power back to Earth.

If O'Neill's plans are followed, this is what we might expect. By the late 1900s or early 2000s, there would be no need to build new power plants on Earth. By 2015, part of Earth's people would be living in space. The population on Earth might even start going down. By 2050, most "dirty" factories would have been moved into space. There, using low-cost power, the materials we waste now will be made over to be used again and again. Once more the Earth would become beautiful!

Perhaps the greatest impact of colonies in space may be in our minds. People will see they are no longer living on a doomed world. With new hope, the changes on Earth may be as sweeping as those in space itself.

UNSCRAMBLE SCIENTIFIC WORDS *vocabulary*

Match each word in Column A with its meaning in Column B.

> *Column A*
> ____ orbit
> ____ gravity
> ____ cylinder
> ____ solar energy
> ____ space
> ____ satellite
> *Column B*

1. weight
2. travel around the earth or some other heavenly body
3. unlimited room that extends in all directions
4. man-made object shot into orbit around the earth or other heavenly body
5. power from the sun
6. long round object

◁ 210 · *Each correct answer 5 points · My Score* ____

ORBITING ANSWERS *skimming*

Underline the ending which best completes each sentence.

1. The cylinder will be spinning to make artificial (a. waves, b. air, c. gravity).

2. When you get near the center of the cylinder, "gravity" (a. decreases, b. increases, c. doesn't exist).

3. Sunlight will stream in through (a. a door, b. long slots, c. a window).

4. Space communities could be ready by around the year (a. 1984, b. 2000, c. 3000).

5. Each cylinder can have its own (a. climate and season, b. pilot, c. color).

6. Ore for building in space will come from (a. the sun, b. the earth, c. the moon).

☞ 180 · Each correct answer 5 points · My Score _____

HOW HIGH IS UP?   *sentence meaning*

Circle the letter of the phrase that best explains the author's meaning in each numbered sentence.

1. Once factories can run in space, the Earth's air and water would start cleaning up.
> a. Using solar energy will reduce pollution.
> b. There will be more room to store garbage.
> c. There will be no people on Earth.

2. Perhaps the greatest impact of colonies in space may be in our minds.
> a. We'll have more room to think.
> b. Space exploration is exciting.
> c. The idea of cities in space gives people hope.

3. This bold plan to put whole colonies in space sounds like science fiction.
> a. It would make a good movie.
> b. It's good to dream.
> c. It doesn't seem possible.

4. Living in this cylinder will have strange effects.
> a. You will be lightheaded.
> b. Much of life will seem topsy-turvy.
> c. You will see Martians.

☞ 89 · Each correct answer 10 points · My Score _____
Perfect Total Score 100 · My Total Score _____

ROCKETING IDEAS   *comparison/contrast*

Imagine what your life might be like if you lived in outer space. In what ways might your life be the same as now? In what ways might it be different?

Karl Krøyer: Inventions to Order

by J. D. Ratcliff

"We inventors are supposed to be an odd lot. But we aren't. Others deal in wheat, stocks or land. We deal in ideas. We fill a place between the dreamers and the engineers." The speaker, Denmark's Karl Krøyer, holds 200 patents and is one of the world's leading inventors.

In his early 60s, Krøyer hardly fits the picture of a poor, wild-haired inventor. He looks more like a successful businessperson—which he is. Neatly dressed, he looks out on the world through horn-rimmed glasses with confident, smiling eyes. He has made several million dollars.

Krøyer gets called in on the strangest kinds of problems. Not long ago, one of Denmark's insurance companies asked him for help. They were worried about

writing policies on buildings with hidden, wood-eating insects. They wanted a quick, easy way to discover the presence of these pests. "Why not listen to them eating?" asked Krøyer. It took him only a few days to make an electronic device that picked up the sound of the insects chewing the inside building beams, while it blocked out all other sounds.

In 1964, when a storm-tossed freighter sank in Kuwait Harbor, Krøyer was presented with the difficult task of raising the ship—a new field to him. Many a ship had been raised before, but not when it lay on its side, as this one did.

Krøyer came up with a striking idea. A certain kind of plastic grows 50 times in size when exposed to steam. Tiny bits swell to pieces the size of BB's. These pieces can float. If the ship were pumped full of this feather-light material, wouldn't it come bobbing to the surface? It was worth a try.

Enough of the particles to fill 100 railroad cars were pumped into the ship. The ship rose slowly to the surface. Cleaned and patched, the vessel is now back in service. Krøyer's idea brought him $186,000, and his method has since been used to raise other ships.

Krøyer's inventive career began when he was a youngster. Krøyer's father manufactured clothes. When Karl was 16 years old, he found a way to improve the fit of women's swimsuits. It was an instant success.

Always observant, he watched his mother in the kitchen. Certain foods stuck in pans because the pans had flat surfaces. So Karl invented a pan with little rounded dents on the bottom. Seven European companies bought this idea, and the young man started getting *royalties* (money for the use of an inventor's idea).

These were just small, beginning ideas for a budding genius. The big things would come later—ideas that have left a mark on world highway building, papermaking, and a number of other projects.

Until a dozen years ago or so, Krøyer worked alone. Then he built a shining steel-and-glass laboratory in Aarhus, Denmark, and hired a team of 100 scientists and engineers. It is one of the few invention factories in the world.

Where does an inventor get ideas? . . . and do a job? "In general," says Krøyer, "we always try to picture needs for new products, or means of improving old ones. We read the magazines and study the marketplace. We listen to what people say about existing goods. In time, inventing becomes a habit."

While many ideas start this way, others come from outside. Several years ago, one of Denmark's road-building companies asked Krøyer if there was any way to color black *asphalt* white—to make it easier for drivers to see the road's surface at night. At first Krøyer thought a simple answer would be to add crushed limestone. But this would soak up oil drippings from cars and soon be black. Also, limestone was soft and would soon wear smooth, making roads dangerously slippery.

Why not mix the asphalt with a light-colored, very hard substance? Krøyer and team went to work. They soon came up with a glasslike substance which, when

mixed with asphalt, makes one of the best paving materials ever discovered. There is less danger of cars skidding on it, and it gives off less headlight glare. Sugar-cube-sized pieces of this white stuff are mixed in with black asphalt, and newly poured roads are black at first. But as asphalt wears away, the top surfaces of Krøyer's stuff shows through, turning roads lighter and brighter. Several thousands of miles of roads in Europe and Japan are paved with it.

The material's uses don't stop there. It can be formed into bricks for home building, and about 3000 homes in Denmark are now made of it. It is also used in public water-treating plants as filters.

What promises to be the most important of all Krøyer's inventions came along not long ago—a "dry" process for making good paper. Today most paper is made by grinding up wood, cotton and so forth. This pulp is then mixed with enormous amounts of water—100 tons (907.2 kilograms) of water to make a ton of paper. (This is why most paper is made in places having huge water resources.) This thin paste then goes into one of the earth's biggest, most costly machines. The principal job of this machine is to get rid of the water! Krøyer felt there must be a better, cheaper way to make paper. Instead of mixing the pulp with water, why not use air to blow the finely ground fibers onto a screen, like snowflakes?

This was the starting point for the new process which will soon go into use in Denmark. A powerful air stream blasts the fibers onto a belt of fine-mesh webbing. Here they are caught and covered with a gluelike binder. Then

the sheet is treated to give any surface desired. It can be made to look and feel like anything from leather to silk.

Turning to road safety, Krøyer has come up with an idea for improving traffic lights. It's simple. A moving spot of light circles the rim of the traffic light like the hand of a watch. It tells the approaching driver how soon the light will change.

Krøyer is now working on another project that will please anyone who cooks. This is a gauge which measures both time and temperature in a single scale. It is to be built into the handles of pots and pans. A small book comes with it telling what the reading should be when any particular food is done.

For obvious reasons, Krøyer doesn't talk much about ideas in the works. But he is willing to talk about one which has interesting possibilities—a room-heating wallpaper! It would be a paper-and-metal sandwich, a thin layer of metal between two sheets of paper. One sheet of paper would serve as wallpaper, the other would soak up noise. Plug the paper into electricity, and the metal would heat up, giving the room an even warmth not possible with most of today's heating equipment.

It's quite a world Krøyer lives in—a world of tomorrow. He is too practical a person to live in the past. The world he sees ahead has better roads to drive on, better foods to eat for better health, new comforts and a galaxy of new products that are not dreamed of today.

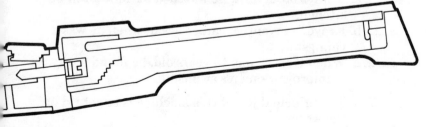

SOLVE THE PROBLEM *classification/outline*

A list of problems Karl Krøyer was given is followed by a list of his solutions—his inventions. Match the problems with the solutions.

Problem

_____ 1. find termites
_____ 2. raise sunken freighter
_____ 3. make white highway
_____ 4. find "dry" process for making paper
_____ 5. prevent food sticking

Solution

a. fill it with plastic that grows
b. blow fibers onto a screen
c. listen to them eating with electronic device
d. pan with rounded dents on bottom
e. mix asphalt with glasslike substance

☞156 · *Each correct answer 10 points · My Score* _____

WHAT'S THE POINT? *main idea*

In each set of sentences below, one sentence gives a main idea and two sentences support it. Check ✔ each main idea.

1._____ a. In his early 60s, Krøyer hardly fits the picture of a poor, wild-haired inventor.
_____ b. Neatly dressed, he looks out on the world through horn-rimmed glasses with confident, smiling eyes.
_____ c. He has made several million dollars.

2._____ a. Always observant, he watched his mother in her kitchen.
_____ b. Krøyer's inventive career began when he was a youngster.
_____ c. When Krøyer was 16 years old, he found a way to improve women's swimsuits.

3._____ a. The principal job of this machine is to get rid of the water.

_____ b. Instead of mixing the pulp with water, the machine uses air to blow the fibers onto a screen.

_____ c. One of Krøyer's most important inventions is a machine for making good paper.

☞ 49 · *Each correct answer 5 points* · *My Score* _____

THE PERSON *characterization*
Put a check ✔ before five words below that can be used to describe Karl Krøyer as he is presented in the selection.

_____ 1. sloppy
_____ 2. careful
_____ 3. poor
_____ 4. observant
_____ 5. creative
_____ 6. successful
_____ 7. wild-haired
_____ 8. practical

☞ 170 · *Each correct answer 5 points* · *My Score* _____

GIVE IT SOME THOUGHT *generalizations*
Underline the best ending for each statement.

1. The story is written in a manner that is (a. informative, b. argumentative, c. funny).

2. The author's main source of information seems to be (a. government reports, b. his own investigations, c. television).

☞ 2 · *Each correct answer 5 points* · *My Score* _____
Perfect Total Score 100 · *My Total Score* _____

BE INVENTIVE *summary*
How does Karl Krøyer get ideas for inventions? Can you think of anything that needs to be invented? Explain.

The Return of the Beaver

by Emily and Ola d'Aulaire

Not long ago, in a small town in Connecticut, an event occurred that is happening all over the United States and Canada. The beaver came back.

Nobody had seen beavers in this town for years. Then, one night, there they were, chewing on maples and willows in a local swamp. By morning trees lay everywhere, looking like a giant game of pickup sticks. Beavers had moved in branches and leaves to plug up a culvert that ran under a road. The water from a stream was supposed to go through the culvert. Instead the road was flooded.

A grate was installed in the culvert to keep the beavers out. But the grate didn't stop the beavers. Soon the road was flooded again. The State Conservation Commission was called in. The beavers had to be trapped and moved away without harming them.

Some people today consider the beaver a troublemaker. But this animal played an important part in North America's early development. Beaver coats and hats were very fashionable at the beginning of the nineteenth century. Trappers blazed trails into the wilderness in search of beaver to skin them for their *pelts*. For a time, beaver pelts even replaced money. One pelt bought a pound (454 grams) of tobacco, twelve pelts bought a rifle.

The pelts that made people rich almost led to the beaver's destruction. By the late 1800s, with the beaver nearly gone, the land began to suffer. Beavers had built dams to trap branches and leaves for food. With no dams, tons of valuable soil washed out to sea. Wells went dry because there were no more beaver-made ponds to provide a new supply of water.

It wasn't until the early 1900s that people fully understood the beaver's importance. Wildlife agencies put the remaining beavers in the woods, where they could increase in numbers and not be harmed. Now beavers are numerous.

The beaver is a perfect building machine. The beaver has hands that can dig and grip. Their large teeth cut through the biggest trees. An adult beaver measures four feet (122 centimeters) and weighs up to 65 pounds (29.4 kilograms). It uses its flat tail like a paddle to thump wood and mud into place. In the water, a beaver is grace and speed. On land, it moves like a clumsy, furry tank.

Before a beaver family chooses a place to live, they spend several days looking it over. They decide which stream won't run dry in summer. They figure out if spring rains will wash the dam away, how much work will result in the largest possible pond.

During the fall, the beavers start to plan their winter *lodge*. In their pond they make an island of branches, sticks and stones. Inside the island they make two or three tunnels that open under water. The outside of the lodge is covered with thick, wet mud. In winter the mud freezes as solid as cement. A hole is left on top to let in fresh air. When the pond freezes, the beavers are trapped for the winter. But they have a store of tender branches in the bottom of the pond.

Beavers live in small, close-knit family groups of parents and *kits* (baby beavers). Bark from trees is a favorite food, and since beavers can't climb trees, the trees must come down. A colony of beavers cuts down as many as 2000 trees a year to build dams. The dams flood an area of woodland, thereby bringing fallen trees into swimmable reach. The whole family helps build and maintain these dams.

How does the beaver know that water flows downhill? How does it know the water can be dammed up? How does it know to build its lodge and put in a supply of winter food? Is the beaver, in fact, smart? Or is all this just instinct, just natural talent?

Experts can't agree. But there are words that describe the beaver—patient, hard-working, energetic. These terms also describe the people of North America. Perhaps we learned some of them from the beaver.

SPEAKING OF BEAVERS *vocabulary*

Write the numeral of the missing word in each sentence below.

A newly born beaver is a _____.
The beaver's family is called a _____.
The skin from a fur-bearing animal is a _____.
A beaver's winter home is known as a _____.
A structure built to block water flow is a _____.

     1. pelt   2. lodge   3. colony   4. kit   5. dam

☞ *167 • Each correct answer 10 points • My Score* _____

WHAT DOES THAT REMIND YOU OF? *figurative language*

Circle the letter of the word groups the author used to give you mental pictures of the following:

1. How the beaver uses its tail
    a. like a flag
    b. like a paddle

2. The way a beaver moves on land
    a. a clumsy, furry tank
    b. a slim, graceful dancer

3. How a beaver's body is designed for reshaping its surroundings
    a. a perfect building machine
    b. a sculptor in the summer woodland

4. The way the fallen trees in the swamp looked
    a. a neat row of pins and needles
    b. a giant game of pickup sticks

5. The mud on the outside of the lodge in winter
    a. as soft as putty
    b. as solid as cement

☞ *129 • Each correct answer 5 points • My Score* _____

FRIEND OR FOE? *inferences*

Each opinion below is either favorable or unfavorable toward the beaver. If the speaker regards the beaver as a friend, write A. If the speaker looks upon the animal as a foe, write B.

A. Friend   B. Foe

_____ 1. "Do you see the lake beyond the barn? That used to be my cornfield."

_____ 2. "The beavers came here ten years ago, and our well hasn't been low on water since then."

_____ 3. "A colony of beavers invaded that stand of aspen trees, and now look at it! There's hardly a tree left."

_____ 4. "When we had a bad dry spell last summer, all the animals in this area depended upon the dammed-up beaver pond to survive."

_____ 5. "Do you know why my crops on this piece of land are so good? A long time ago, one beaver dam was built on top of the other. When the beavers moved on and the ponds dried up, a thick layer of rich topsoil was left."

☞ *130 · Each correct answer 5 points · My Score* _____
Perfect Total Score 100 · My Total Score _____

THE BEAVER IS NOT ALONE *fact/opinion*

Can you think of other animals besides the beaver that some people see as friend and foe? Explain.

How do you regard the following creatures—the alligator, the wolf, the vulture, and the bee? Give reasons for your answer.

KING TUT'S GOLDEN TREASURE

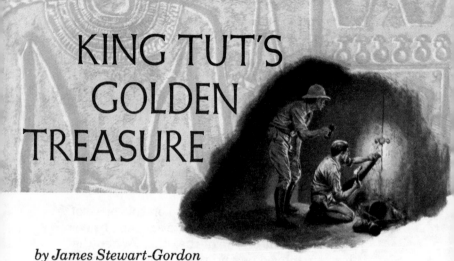

by James Stewart-Gordon

Two men, tense with excitement, stood before a sealed door. The door, they believed, had not been opened for more than 3000 years. Behind it lay a treasure beyond dreams—or else an empty room.

It was November 26, 1922. The door was at the end of a passage cut in the limestone rock in Egypt's Valley of the Kings.

Howard Carter had searched for this door for many years. His companion, Lord Carnarvon, had spent a fortune backing him. If the lost tomb of King Tutankha- mon (TOOT-ahngk-AH-mun) was not beyond the door, they could no longer afford to search.

Cautiously Carter worked at the plaster that sealed

the door, while Carnarvon peered over his shoulder. As plaster crumbled under Carter's tapping, the excitement mounted. Bit by bit, the hole grew wider, until at last Carter could shine a candle in.

At first Carter could see nothing. A rush of hot air escaped from the sealed room, causing his candle flame to flicker. But slowly his eyes became used to the dim light. He later wrote, "Details of the room within emerged slowly from the mist, strange animals, statues, and gold—everywhere the glint of gold. For the moment—an eternity it must have seemed to the others standing by—I was struck dumb with amazement."

At last Carnarvon whispered anxiously, "Can you see anything?"

Carter could barely get out the words, "Yes, wonderful things. . . ."

He widened the hole so that both could peer into the tomb. Their light flickered over a pink room 26 feet (8.6 meters) by 12 feet (4 meters). First its rays shone on three golden couches, carved in the shape of animals with huge heads. Then the moving light showed two life-sized statues of men, facing each other before another sealed door. Each armed guard carried a staff and wore on his forehead a cobra—a sacred snake in ancient Egypt.

Everywhere the light moved it showed wonders— beautiful boxes and jars, gold beds, carved chairs, musical instruments, a gold throne ablaze with colored stones. Here was a view of life in Egypt more than 1300 years before the birth of Christ.

What lay beyond the sealed door guarded by the two statues? The greatest treasure of all—the burial room. Four wooden shrines coated with gold enclosed a nest of four coffins, the innermost one of solid gold. In it lay the mummy of 18-year-old King Tutankhamon. The carefully wrapped body wore a mask of pure gold, inlaid with fine blue glass, and a collar of real flowers. Although withered, the flowers still had a faint color. King Tutankhamon's young queen may have placed them there just before the coffin was closed.

The world in 1922 went crazy over Tutankhamon. Overnight he became "King Tut." Newspaper reporters flocked to Egypt. Tourists swarmed over the Valley of the Kings like ants.

It took ten years for Carter and other scholars to carefully remove, record and preserve all the treasures. When at last these went on view in the Cairo museum, they delighted thousands of visitors—just as they still do today.

The dramatic story of the finding of the tomb still fascinates the world. It is mainly Howard Carter's story.

When Carter, an Englishman, was 17, his talent for drawing got him a job. He went to Egypt, where he copied drawings for an archaeologist—a scientist who studies the remains of the past. In time, Carter himself studied archaeology.

At 26, he became an inspector of ancient monuments in Egypt. It was then that he became interested in King Tutankhamon.

Most of the tombs of the great kings of Egypt had been robbed of their treasures. But nothing was known of Tutankhamon's tomb. Then, in 1907, a few pieces of gold leaf were found. Tutankhamon's name had been pressed into the gold. Later another archaeologist, digging in the Valley of the Kings, found a few jars containing straw, animal bones, and other bits of trash. These, it was later learned, had been used at Tutankhamon's burial. But at the time, the archaeologist didn't think them important enough to study.

Where was Tutankhamon's tomb? And why had nothing from his tomb ever turned up in the market? Carter was fascinated with these questions. He knew that tomb robbers sold anything they found. If none of the king's treasures had ever come to light, perhaps the tomb—wherever it was—had never been robbed!

From then on, Carter searched for the tomb. In 1907, he and Lord Carnarvon formed a company. More than anything, Carter wanted to dig in the Valley of the Kings. But only one person—the archaeologist who had found the jars—had permission to do so. For a while Carter dug in other places. He and Lord Carnarvon made some interesting discoveries—but not the great discovery of their dreams.

Then, in 1914, the other archaeologist gave up his digging and went home! Immediately Carter and Carnarvon asked for permission to dig in the Valley of the Kings. They got it—but the officer who signed their papers told them they were wasting their time.

It seemed the officer was right. Disappointment followed disappointment. War broke out, and the two men could not begin their digging. Three years later, when Carter did begin work, there was very little to find. Many places in the Valley of the Kings had already been dug up. One spot interested Carter very much—but it was right on the pathway to a large and famous tomb. Rather than block the path of the visitors, Carter passed it by. He spent years digging in other parts of the valley. His workers moved thousands of tons of sand and rock—and found almost nothing.

Finally, early in 1922, Lord Carnarvon called Carter to England. Carter would have to give up the search, he said. They had already spent a fortune, with no results.

Throne of gold, silver and jewels

Lotus-flower cup *Golden goddess standing guard*

Gilded statue *Wooden dog with silver claws and jeweled eyes*

Carter begged for one last try. He could not get the spot by the pathway out of his mind. At last Carnarvon agreed—to one more try.

Carter went back to Egypt early, to beat the stream of winter visitors that came to the Valley of the Kings. In three days he and his workers dug up the pathway. Only a thin layer of dirt was left above solid rock.

When Carter arrived at the digging on November 4, he knew something important had been found. Usually the workers sang and talked as they dug—but now they were silent. They stepped aside and showed him what they had found—a step cut into the ground.

By the next day, the digging had revealed a sunken stairway and a sealed door. Carter felt in his bones that the search was almost over.

He ordered the work stopped. Then he sent a cable to Lord Carnarvon: "AT LAST HAVE MADE WONDERFUL DISCOVERY IN VALLEY. A MAGNIFICENT TOMB WITH SEALS INTACT. RE-COVERED SAME FOR YOUR ARRIVAL. CONGRATULATIONS."

Carnarvon left immediately for Egypt. Excitedly he watched the digging with Carter. At last they opened the outer door.

The passage beyond it was filled with rocks, put there by the builders of the tomb to discourage robbers. At the end of the passage was another sealed door. And behind that door lay the wonders of King Tutankhamon's golden treasure.

WHAT DOES IT SAY?   *paragraph meaning*

Circle the letter of the answer that tells about each
paragraph. Be sure to read the whole paragraph first.

1. At first Carter could see nothing. (page 89, paragraph 1)
   a. Nothing was in the tomb.
   b. Carter was amazed at what he saw in the room.
   c. A rush of hot air escaped from the room.

2. What lay beyond the sealed door guarded by the two
statues? (page 89, paragraph 6)
   a. Two statues guarded the sealed door.
   b. The flowers still had a faint color.
   c. They had found the greatest treasure of all—King
      Tutankhamon's burial room.

3. It seemed the officer was right. (page 92, paragraph 4)
   a. Carter worked hard in the Valley of the Kings, but
      found nothing important.
   b. After war broke out, the men had to begin their
      work.
   c. Many visitors used the path to the tomb.

⟜ *52 · Each correct answer 5 points · My Score* _____

SKIM FOR FACTS   *skimming*

Put a check ✔ before four things that were found in
Tutankhamon's tomb.

_____ 1. three golden couches
_____ 2. musical instruments
_____ 3. gold beads
_____ 4. some real flowers
_____ 5. a real snake
_____ 6. Tutankhamon's mummy

⟜ *123 · Each correct answer 5 points · My Score* _____

WORDS AND MEANINGS   *vocabulary*

Read each sentence below. Look at the word in italics.
Which word below has a similar meaning? Put the letter of
that word next to the sentence.

_____ *Cautiously* Carter worked at the plaster that sealed the door.

_____ Although *withered,* the flowers still had a faint color.

_____ It took ten years to remove, record and *preserve* all the treasures.

A. protect   C. wilted
B. carefully   D. clumsily

☞ 52 · *Each correct answer 5 points · My Score* _____

THE ARCHAEOLOGIST   *characterization*

Before each sentence below, put the letter of the word that best describes how Howard Carter felt at the time.

A. amazed   B. determined   C. curious
D. disappointed   E. excited

_____ What lay beyond the sealed door guarded by the two statues?

_____ Details of the room within emerged slowly from the mist, strange animals, statues, and gold—everywhere the glint of gold.

_____ Then he sent a cable to Lord Carnarvon: "AT LAST HAVE MADE WONDERFUL DISCOVERY IN VALLEY."

_____ He spent years digging in other parts of the valley.

_____ Carter would have to give up the search. They had already spent a fortune, with no results.

☞ 156 · *Each correct answer 10 points · My Score* _____
Perfect Total Score 100 · My Total Score _____

THE DISCOVERY   *generalization*

What made the discovery of Tutankhamon's tomb so exciting? Why was Carter successful when others had failed?